3/22/04 Inh marks. Bc

D1014842

pencil
when not
3-14-04
LF

LISTENING
MADE *EASY*

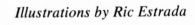
Illustrations by Ric Estrada

LISTENING
MADE *EASY*

How to Improve Listening
on the Job, at Home,
and in the Community

ROBERT L. MONTGOMERY

A Division of American Management Associations

BF
323
.L5
M58

Dedicated to the three greatest women in my life:

My mother, Vina Marie,
My wife, Carmen Dolores,
My daughter, Marie Cyr.

All three are exemplary listeners who motivated me to improve my own listening ability and then to help others improve theirs.

Library of Congress Cataloging in Publication Data

Montgomery, Robert Leo, 1927–
  Listening made easy.

  Includes index.
  1. Listening. I. Title.
BF323.L5M58   001.54'2   80-69689
ISBN 0-8144-5650-2   AACR2

© 1981 AMACOM
A division of American Management Associations, New York.
All rights reserved. Printed in the United States of America.

This publication may not be reproduced, stored in a retrieval system, or transmitted in whole or in part, in any form or by any means, electronic, mechanical, photocopying, recording, or otherwise, without the prior written permission of AMACOM, 135 West 50th Street, New York, N.Y. 10020.

First Printing.

10/5/81
65363

Preface

*Man's inability to communicate is a result
of his failure to listen effectively, skillfully,
and with understanding to another person.*
—Carl Rogers

Do you listen to others as you like to be listened to? It takes skill and determination to speak, but it takes even more skill and determination to listen to others. It also takes energy. Harrel T. Allen, a communications expert, reports: "Listening is hard work and requires increased energy. Your heart speeds up, your blood circulates faster, your temperature goes up."

We listen more than we do any other human activity except breathe. Listening is essential to our personal, professional, social, and family success. If working people were taught to listen effectively, the efficiency of American business could be doubled.

Listening is the most neglected and the least understood of the communications arts. It has become the weakest link in today's communications system. Poor listening is a result of bad habits that develop because we haven't been trained to listen. Fortunately, it is a skill that can be learned. A major company—Sperry Corporation—recently proclaimed in a series of full-page newspaper ads: "How can we expect our children to learn if we haven't taught them to listen?"

Poor listening is a twentieth-century epidemic. The latest saying is, "No one listens to anyone anymore. And if you listen for a while, you'll understand why." People drone on with slow speech, poor vocabulary, and bad grammar. Speakers are guilty of mumbling, rambling, repeating; their tone is nasal, their pitch a monotone. Listeners are guilty of tuning out; yielding to distractions; becoming overemotional; faking attention; allowing mental detours and private planning; or even dozing with their eyes open.

Taylor Caldwell highlights the problem in her novel *The Listener.* "The most desperate need of men today is not a new vaccine for any disease, or a new religion, or a new 'way of life.' Man does not need to go to the moon or other solar systems. He does not require bigger and better bombs and missiles. . . . His real need, his most terrible need, is for someone to listen to him, not as a 'patient' but as a human soul."

A *Reader's Digest* author stated, "People don't

need a doctor. They need an audience: just one interested listener."

With a little knowledge and practice you can double your listening ability. My first objective in writing this book is to help you discover the importance of listening to gain a life of greater happiness and success. My second and major objective is to provide the principles and rules that, with practice, can increase your listening ability 100 percent.

Listening is a gift you can give, no matter who you are. And you can give it to anyone. It doesn't cost a cent, but it is priceless to a person who needs a listener.

Wherever you are, you can start today to learn to listen.

Albert Camus provides an inspirational thought to stimulate our desire to be better listeners: "Great ideas, it has been said, come into the world as gently as doves. Perhaps, then, if we listen attentively, we shall hear amid the uproar of empires and nations a faint flutter of wings, the gentle stirring of life and hope."

Robert L. Montgomery

Contents

1
Introduction to Total Listening

If you're talking,
you aren't learning.
—Lyndon Johnson

UNDERSTANDING THE PROBLEM

It was an early spring evening. A good friend of mine was flying south out of New York City on a Delta airliner. One of the stewardesses got the passengers' attention through the intercom system:

"Ladies and gentlemen, children too, we're going to play a game and give away some prizes. About 15 minutes ago, just after we took off from Kennedy airport, the captain spoke over the intercom. He gave his name and also some information about the flight.

1

Our first prize will be given to the passenger who is first to answer a question. Just push the call button above if you know the answer. We're going to test and see how well you listened.

"First question. What is the captain's name? That was the first thing he announced. Push the call button if you know."

My friend reported that none of the more than 100 passengers could answer the question. Not one person could recall a name spoken loud and clear just 15 minutes earlier. The problem is not so much one of memory as one of concentrated listening. The art of *retention* is dependent upon the art of *attention*.

The biggest problem in listening is this: We fail to focus on the other person's point of view or idea. It's human nature to want to tell our ideas, feelings, opinions, convictions, and jokes. And we want to tell our own thoughts instantly—without even waiting until the other person has finished talking. We interrupt and often change the subject at the same time. Most people are egocentric, and this contributes to poor listening.

How is *your* listening ability? How often do you have to ask people to repeat something they just said? How often do you have to say "Pardon me?" when speaking with others? How well do you hear and remember names?

We know that people's retention improves with their ability to be active listeners. Concentrated attention breeds good retention.

Probably the greatest example of the poor listening

ability of Americans occurred on Sunday night, October 30, 1938, between 8:15 and 9:30 P.M. when the Columbia Broadcasting System and its affiliated stations presented Orson Welles and the *Mercury Theatre* on the air in *The War of the Worlds* by H. G. Wells.

This dramatization of Wells's fantasy led thousands to believe an interplanetary conflict had started, with invading Martians spreading death and destruction across New Jersey and New York. The broadcast caused a nightmare for many Americans because although they were listening, they didn't hear.

The broadcast, which disrupted households, interrupted religious services, created traffic jams, and clogged communications systems, was produced and narrated by Orson Welles who, as the radio character "The Shadow," used to give the creeps to countless child listeners. This time at least a score of adults required medical attention for shock and hysteria.

In Newark, New Jersey, in a single block at Heddon Terrace and Hawthorne Avenue, more than 20 families rushed out of their houses with wet handkerchiefs and towels over their faces to flee from what they believed to be a gas raid. Some began moving household furniture.

Throughout New York, families left their homes, some to flee to nearby parks. Thousands of persons called the police, newspapers, and radio stations in New York and in other cities of the United States and Canada seeking advice on protective measures against the raids.

The radio play was presented to simulate a regular

radio program, with a "break-in" for the material of the play. The radio listeners apparently missed or did not listen to the introduction, which was: "The Columbia Broadcasting System and its affiliated stations present Orson Welles and the *Mercury Theatre* on the air in *The War of the Worlds* by H. G. Wells." Listeners also failed to associate the program with the newspaper listing of the dramatization and ignored or simply didn't hear three additional announcements made during the broadcast emphasizing its fictional nature.

That's the story. A real incident that actually occurred—one that involved poor listening and overly emotional reactions on the part of many U.S. citizens.

Edmond G. Addeo and Robert E. Burger, in their book *Egospeak,** say, "The reason that no one listens, usually, is that our egos get in the way in the sense that we're mentally formulating what *we're* going to say as soon as the other person gets through speaking." These authors also believe, "If someone speaks and no one listens, there has been no communication."

Bartenders are man's best friend, because they are obliged to listen eight hours a day to other people's problems. For psychiatrists and clergymen, their job is listening to people's problems and counseling them; most of them are overworked. I overheard one woman say recently, "Everybody loves to talk and nobody wants to listen. No wonder so many people are seeing psychiatrists."

*New York: Bantam Books, 1973.

Communication is to love what blood is to life. Abraham Schmitt, author of *The Art of Listening with Love,** says that good listening can transform people and relationships. "This kind of listening," he says, "can free the speaker to search deeper and deeper for a more full understanding and admiration of himself. Listening is then a great act of love at that moment, for it makes the other person more whole."

KEY CAUSES OF POOR LISTENING

The problem today is not one of getting men and women to talk, it's one of getting men and women to listen. Many people have had some kind of speech or communications training, but scarcely anyone has ever had any kind of training in how to listen. Poor listening stems from bad habits, which exist, even abound, because we've not been trained.

Bad habits include listening for facts only, daydreaming, disliking the speaker, private planning, overemotional responses, mental detours, debating, tuning out too soon, and avoiding complex or technical material. In addition to bad habits and lack of training, endless distractions interfere with good listening. Distractions range from anger to laziness to self-consciousness to a toothache. Sometimes these distractions are called barriers.

You can become a better listener, however. It's possible to improve your listening ability almost 100

*Waco, Tex.: Word Books, 1977.

percent as soon as you start to practice the principles of active listening you'll learn in this book. Most people use only about 25 percent of their native ability for listening. Somehow, in the past, we've neglected the art of listening in our educational requirements.

More elementary schools, high schools, and colleges, as well as sponsors of adult education courses and seminars, are now including training in listening. This book highlights the material I've developed over 26 years of teaching courses for executives and students. I've taught for colleges and universities, American Management Associations, and a long list of blue-chip corporation clients.

The University of Minnesota reports that, in the business world, nearly 60 percent of misunderstanding can be traced to poor listening and only 1 percent to written communication. Yet one management expert declared, "Listening is the manager's prime tool for managing. To manage, it's necessary to know your subordinates and understand them. It's important to know each individual's needs, problems, and goals. The only way to discover them is through questioning and listening." Leadership is practically impossible for the person who can't listen effectively.

In the home, poor listening leads the list of causes of marital conflict. In a nationwide survey conducted by the Family Service Association of America, husbands and wives were asked, "What are the major conflicts in your married life?"

Eighty-seven percent said, "Poor communication"

or "No communication." "My spouse doesn't listen to me" was the reason most frequently given.

Forty-six percent said, "Children." "My children don't listen to me" and "My children don't do what I tell them" were the major reasons cited.

Forty-four percent said, "Sex." Surprisingly, the word *communication* was frequently in the response.

Finally, 37 percent said, "Money." Certainly, with inflation and higher taxes and exploding prices for homes, cars, and gasoline, this problem must be an increasing source of conflict.

Still, no conflict comes even close to the biggest troublemaker of all in family life—poor communication, particularly poor listening. Children and young people I've taught in schools and courses frequently remark, "My parents don't listen to me. They don't care." As one small child said, "My father and I had words this morning, but I didn't get to use mine." Children have little opportunity for the give and take of a real conversation with adults, because adults talk *to* them, not *with* them. This defines the generation gap as the communications gap.

It is evident that poor listening is a problem between employees and bosses, children and parents, and husbands and wives. Misunderstandings are like automobile accidents—they're always the other person's fault. How often do you hear someone take the blame? The answer is rarely, if ever. Is it any wonder there have been 1 million divorces each year in the United States since 1975?

To repeat, the single biggest cause of poor listening is the failure to concentrate on the other person's point of view or ideas. We engage in passive instead of total listening.

In his essay "How to Attend a Conference," Senator S. I. Hayakawa of California writes:

Few people . . . have had much training in listening. Living in a competitive culture, most of us are most of the time chiefly concerned with getting our own views across, and we tend to find other people's speeches a tedious interruption of the flow of our own ideas.

Hence it is necessary to emphasize that listening does not mean simply maintaining a polite silence while you are rehearsing in your mind the speech you are going to make the next time you can grab a conversation opening. Nor does listening mean waiting alertly for the flaws in the other person's argument so that later you can mow him or her down. Listening means trying to see the problem the way the speaker sees it. . . . Listening requires entering actively and imaginatively into the other person's situation and trying to understand a frame of reference different than your own.

Are you a good listener? Are you eager to learn about other people, places, and things? Do you ever ask for feedback on how people rate you as a listener? Do you work to identify the main ideas, attitudes, and feelings being communicated? Do you avoid interrupting? Especially, do you curb the impulse to complete the other person's sentences?

Can you put yourself in the other person's shoes? Do you tune in to the speaker's feelings as well as the words being spoken? Do you try to overcome your own emotional attitudes and prejudgments? Do you consciously practice listening skills?

Real communication occurs when we listen with understanding. This brings us to the main objectives of communication: (1) to be deeply understanding of others; (2) to be clearly understood; (3) to be accepted by others; and (4) to get action. The word *motivation* comes from words that mean "to move to action."

The words are simple, the task is tough. Deeply understanding others requires total listening and skillful questioning. Everything in this book is designed to help you improve your understanding of others through concentrated listening. But listening is hard work, and it is complicated because of interference from emotions, bias, personality traits, and distractions. It takes thinking. And as Ralph Waldo Emerson said, "Thinking is the hardest thing in the world to do."

James Cribbin, management consultant, states that all his experiences show that "*not one person in ten thousand is really interested in trying to understand you and me.*" Yet, the essence of management is to get things done through other people. This takes clear communication. More than half the manager's time is spent listening, but few managers have been trained to listen. Most white-collar workers spend half their time listening to others: in person one to one, in meetings, and on the phone. It could be said that most workers receive half their paycheck for listening. Still, few companies pay any attention to providing training in better listening.

The essence of communication is participation. This means that feedback should be encouraged in delegation, meetings, and all business communication. There is no oral communication unless someone listens, hears, and understands. Sometimes we listen but don't really hear. And sometimes we hear but don't really understand. Training is the answer. Training in listening will help assure understanding.

The key to better listening is you. Each individual must develop the ability of concentrated listening. You owe it to yourself to work hard at improving. First, make it your goal to be a better listener. Desire for improvement is essential. Then make a resolution to be the one person deeply interested in trying to understand others. We're talking now about human understanding. And human understanding depends almost entirely on effective communication, effective listening.

People may be skillful at their work but poor in dealing with others. Promotions to executive positions are usually determined as much on interpersonal as on technical competence.

Listening to others is one of the nonfinancial incentives for motivation. Psychologists tell us that a fundamental principle of human nature is the desire to be appreciated. Listening is one of the highest forms of appreciation you can show another person. Listening completely will help us understand one another, and understanding breeds respect and motivation.

From this kind of human motivation we can expect increased productivity. And that's one goal of this book: increased productivity for yourself and those within reach of your influence. The Department of Labor defines productivity as output per person per hour. In short, we're talking about utilizing our time more productively.

PURPOSE MAKES A DIFFERENCE

Why are some people very good listeners and others poor listeners? One key difference is purpose. We need a definite purpose, a specific reason for listening, otherwise we don't pay attention and don't really hear or understand. Listening is best when purposeful. Here are some possible reasons to motivate yourself to listen more actively:

To be an interested, helpful manager.
To obtain news, facts, or other information.
To form an opinion or reach a decision.
To discover someone's attitude.
To obtain feedback or a response from someone.
To be a friend.

Remember, having an objective or purpose will spark a deeper desire to listen to others.

There is little correlation between IQ and listening. Some people with high IQs flunk the listening test. Others with lower IQs have outstanding listening ability. It's a matter of desire and concentration. After that, it's a matter of eliminating bad habits and replacing them with positive aids to make it easy for you to become a superior listener.

2
Are You
a Good Listener?

Nature has given to man one tongue,
but two ears, that we may hear from others
twice as much as we speak.

—Epictetus

LISTENING, whether with the eyes, ears, or heart, is getting inside the other person and seeing things from his or her point of view. But most people fail to see things from the other person's point of view.

Every time I conduct a course or workshop in effective listening, I begin by asking the participating executives what they think their No. 1 goal is in the course. Here is a list of the most frequently stated objectives.

1. To keep from tuning out.
2. To understand clearly.
3. To be able to recall what I hear.
4. To hear accurately.
5. To listen better after lunch.
6. To turn others off who talk on and on.
7. To concentrate better on what's being said.
8. To curb distractions.
9. To increase my attention span.
10. To keep attentive in meetings.
11. To listen better to my spouse and children.

To this list should be added the desire of teachers, consultants, and interviewers to hear better and not make assumptions about the people they work with.

CHARACTERISTICS OF POOR LISTENERS

Once we've identified our goals, which invariably reflect our problems, we can start improving our listening. As the inventor Charles Kettering said, "A problem well stated is already half solved."

Next, I ask the participants to think of the worst listener they know and state the characteristics of that person. The usual replies are:

1. Always interrupts.
2. Jumps to conclusions.
3. Finishes my sentences.
4. Is inattentive; has wandering eyes and poor posture.
5. Changes the subject.

6. Writes everything down.
7. Doesn't give any response.
8. Is impatient.
9. Loses temper.
10. Fidgets with pen or pencil or paper clip nervously.

CHARACTERISTICS OF GOOD LISTENERS

Then I ask the members of the group to think of the best listeners they know and identify their key traits. The usual answers are:

1. Looks at me while I'm speaking.
2. Questions me to clarify what I'm saying.
3. Shows concern by asking questions about my feelings.
4. Repeats some of the things I say.
5. Doesn't rush me.
6. Is poised and emotionally controlled.
7. Reacts responsively with a nod of the head, a smile, or a frown.
8. Pays close attention.
9. Doesn't interrupt me.
10. Keeps on the subject till I've finished my thoughts.

EVALUATE YOURSELF

Socrates said, "Know thyself. The unexamined life is not worth living." Take a little time to analyze your personal listening habits. Use the lists of characteristics presented above to help you discover your problems and needs. Then make a list of the problems you want to overcome in your daily listening. Be objective and honest. You'll get much more out of this book and improve much faster if you can identify and write down your bad habits and objectives. Ask yourself:

1. How do I see myself as a listener? Be specific.
2. How do others (spouse, friends, children, co-workers) see me as a listener?
3. What kind of communications climate do I create around me at the office and at home? Do people come to me openly with problems?
4. Am I a willing listener who doesn't rush others?
5. Am I easy to talk to?
6. Do I draw out opposite views to fully understand the feelings of others?

Once you've answered these questions through your own introspection and by speaking to others who know you well, write everything down on a master sheet. Keep it handy as a profile to help you accentuate the positive and eliminate the negative. Later chapters will help you find out how to improve.

SOBERING STATISTICS

Studies by the Audio Visual Society have shown that among the major skills listening is way out front as the one we use most each day. The figures show that we listen about 45 percent of our waking hours; we talk about 30 percent of the time; we read around 16 percent of the day; and we write only about 9 percent of the time. Yet, in school we are taught more about writing and less about listening than any of the other skills. And even though we speak much more than we read, speech is not taught as much as reading.

It could be argued that our educational system has its priorities backward. We are taught these four skills in exactly the opposite proportion to the percentage we use them.

Will this problem be corrected? We have to hope so. However, there are more signs of change coming from industry and independent sources than from the schools.

Sperry Corporation has launched a multi-million-dollar advertising campaign to alert the public and educate its 87,000 employees worldwide through courses and audio cassettes. Their full-page newspaper ads in huge bold, black letters, carry the theme: IT'S ABOUT TIME WE LEARNED HOW TO LISTEN. The Ford Motor Company slogan is "We listen better"; 3M says "We hear you."

Independent consultants and educational organizations have started to include training in listening in their programs for management. These same sources are also now producing audio cassettes, films, and books to help train people in the art of listening.

HOPEFUL SIGNS

Recently I found a school paper on my front lawn. It bore the name of a neighbor, seven-year-old Neda. I picked it up simply to throw it away. It was wet, but I

17

noticed the fine printing of the second-grade young-ster. In large print she had written four personal goals:

1. Be a super skater.
2. Be a better reader.
3. Be a good girl.
4. Be a super listener.

The teacher had written in ink on the page: "Great resolutions!"

It was heartening to discover a seven-year-old in-cluding the goal of better listening along with goals for sports, school, and daily life. It reminded me of the nursery schools in the United States that are training preschool youngsters to listen and to share, difficult tasks for all of us but especially for three- and four-year-old children.

At a party not too long after this, an 85-year-old millionaire in my hometown asked me, "What is the secret for being a good listener?" I responded in-stantly, "There is no secret. It's hard work. It takes energy, concentration, and thinking." "But," I added, "it does help to bite your tongue."

Then, as I paused and thought for a moment, I realized the secret is to ask questions, especially open-ended questions that require detailed answers. The elderly gentleman's question had prompted me to speak and enabled him to learn something. A later chapter will cover the art of questioning.

It was refreshing and encouraging to have a young-ster's and an octogenarian's interest displayed in the same month, all while writing this book to make listening easier for everyone.

Also, in the past two years, the heads of government in two countries in opposite parts of the world, Iran and Nicaragua, were literally kicked out of their countries. Both were accused of being lax in listening to the citizens at large and both were overthrown by the masses rising up and marching against them and their armies.

The citizens wanted to be heard, and no one would listen and respond. Hundreds died in each country in the fight for what they hoped would be a more democratic regime.

The lesson to be learned from children, senior citizens, and uprising nations is that the best way to understand people is to listen to them. Now let's get started learning how best to improve our listening ability.

3
Start to Double Your Listening Ability

If you love to listen, you will gain knowledge
and if you incline your ear,
you will become wise.

—Sirach

LISTENING PAYS

Salespeople in the top 10 percent of any company will tell you that super listening put them where they are. It's a well-known fact that in most companies about 20 percent of the salespeople sell around 80 percent of the company's products or services each year. The main difference between salespeople in most instances is that the successful salespeople are good listeners.

Psychiatrists were among the first both to discover

the powers of active or total listening and to show the way to basic and advanced listening techniques. Psychiatrists average about $100 an hour, and the heart of their work is listening.

Parents who take time to listen to their children, which means to get to know them, who help them regularly and do things with them, are apt to be rewarded with greater love and fewer problems of alcohol, drugs, cheating, stealing, or runaway children than parents who do not.

Teachers and bosses who listen can't help but do better in training or managing those in their charge. Where there is better listening there is always better motivation and productivity, whether in school or on the job.

Even talk show hosts are rewarded for one thing mainly: their listening ability. Johnny Carson, Mike Douglas, and Merv Griffin are all paid in the range of $2 million a year for questioning and listening. Asking the right kinds of questions—questions that don't evoke monosyllabic answers—is a prerequisite for anyone who aspires to be a listener instead of a talker. Barbara Walters, Mike Wallace, and others are also in the big money for their ability to question and listen.

WRITE IT DOWN

Albert Einstein told a nephew in a letter that his nephew could recognize him because he always had a pen or pencil in his hand. He did his thinking on paper, where he could see what he was thinking. Psychologists tell us that 83–87 percent of everything that comes into the brain comes through the eyes and only about 11 percent comes through the ears. So you greatly improve your chances of learning by simply seeing what you are interested in learning.

The suggestion then is to write down the essentials of what you hear in a classroom, speech, report, meeting, or anywhere that communication is important. It's wise to obtain a business card from new acquaintances, this saves you writing down their names, phone numbers, businesses, and addresses. Still, it's good to write down any information necessary for follow-up. You can even write it on the back of the business card.

The Presidents Association of New York has long taught executives in their training courses that a person can get 15 percent more out of any communication by asking questions and 20 percent more by taking notes of the key ideas, the essence of the information being given. Also, they teach that any person can gain and retain an additional 35 percent of the communication by making a report on the information provided. Put together the three suggestions—for questioning, taking notes, and writing a report later—and you can learn 70 percent more from any oral communication, even information provided through film, cassettes, radio, or television.

Therefore, always be prepared to write down the key ideas you hear especially during phone conversations, since you can't see the person you're speaking to. Being prepared means having a pen or pencil handy. It means having the right kind of material to write on, preferably a large pad of paper. Many people can write in a more organized way with lined paper, but the preference is personal. The methods for note taking, however, are standard.

HOW TO OUTLINE ORAL COMMUNICATIONS

Now you're ready with pencil or pen, paper, and a decision to outline what you hear in a speech or phone conversation, person to person, or in a meeting or conference. The idea is to write down the essence of what you hear and to learn more and retain it better by seeing it on paper.

Sometimes it will be easy. The speaker may be so organized that you merely have to write down the key points he or she highlights. For example, if I tell you I will share five possible ways to save money on your income tax, you will simply have to write down the five points as I explain them and add the essence of the details I present.

Teachers and speakers often use acronyms to organize their presentations and make them easier to remember. If I give a talk on how to be a better listener and provide six key phrases the first letters of which spell out the acronym L A D D E R (see Chapter 5), you merely have to write out the key phrases. If I tell you the names of the five Great Lakes and list them so they spelled out H O M E S, it will be much easier for you to write them down in a logical and almost unforgettable way: Huron, Ontario, Michigan, Erie, Superior.

24

But, you ask, what about the unorganized speaker or teacher. What then? Answer: Do the best you can. Listen for the key ideas, if any, and use a number, letter, or acronym system you develop as you listen. The point is to capture the main ideas or principles for the essence of the communication.

Good listeners ask themselves questions, such as "Is this speaker organized?" "What is the pattern or method of organization?" Or, if the speaker is unorganized, "How can I best organize this message?"

One of the worst habits of poor listeners is that they tune out to avoid the challenge of thinking and concentrating on difficult material for a sustained period. Why? They have had little or no training in how to listen and are accustomed to written communications in school. It is usually detailed subject matter they tune out, even if it is coming over TV or radio. Poor listeners skip or dodge lectures or commentary. Good listeners, however, seek out educational lectures and programs wherever they are offered. Poor listeners will have to work hard at outlining the communications they hear if they want to overcome the tendency to tune out when the speech content is detailed.

The more one works at hearing and understanding a presentation, the easier it becomes to outline it. Do it once, and you can do it again. Do it twice, and you can make a positive habit out of it. Now I offer a little help in how to outline the more difficult information you hear from any source.

Most writers, reporters, speakers, and teachers follow a system of organization: chronological; analyt-

---

Thoughts About Listening

"The art of listening needs its highest development in listening to oneself; our most important task is to develop an ear that can really hear what we're saying."
—Sidney Harris, columnist

"One friend, one person who is truly understanding, who takes the trouble to listen to us as we consider our problems, can change our whole outlook on the world."
—Elton Mayo, behavioral scientist

"When a person knows that he has a good listener to talk to, he'll share his thoughts more fully, which in turn, makes it easier for the caseworker to help him with his problems. And, moreover, as he talks, the person needing help often finds a good solution to his problems himself."
—Florence Hollis, social worker

"If I can listen to what he tells me, if I can understand how it seems to him, if I can sense the emotional flavor which it has for him, then I will be releasing potent forces of change within him."
—Carl Rogers, psychologist

---

ical; order of importance; comparison and contrast; problem and solution; numerical; alphabetical; and spatial. By understanding these key types of order, you can more easily outline all oral communications. Here's a brief description of each type.

Chronological order is arranged according to time, such as the history of a company, the story of your life since birth, or the listing of events or activities in sequence, such as a witness's explanation in court of how an accident happened. Analytical provides answers to the questions what? where? when? who? and perhaps why? how? and even how many? how much? or how often? Order of importance begins with the most important ideas first. Comparison and contrast demonstrates the differences or similarities between two ideas, concepts, or philosophies such as the Republican and Democratic parties. Problem and solution first highlights the problem and then suggests possible solutions. Numerical and simply alphabetical list the points being made by number or letter. Spatial orders things by their position in space, such as the rooms in your house or the kingdoms of Disneyland.

Study these key methods of arrangement. Remember that a speaker may combine two or more of these types of organization. As a listener, your task is to determine the type or types of arrangement and choose a suitable technique for note taking.

For example, a speaker is giving a lecture titled "Changing Concepts in Communication." He explains he will cite three changing concepts and provide supporting evidence. He relates one concept at a time, followed by specific illustrations and statistics. You can outline the key ideas and supporting data by combining numerical and alphabetical styles. It might look like this when the speaker has finished:

Changing Concepts in Communication

I. The Impact of Visual Aids
   A. As much as 85 percent of what we learn comes through the eyes.
   B. The number one visual aid is *you*.

II. The Importance of Behavioral Communication
   A. Everything by which you and I extend ourselves is communications: face, voice, posture, example, language.
   B. Behavior manifests belief.
   C. People respond to the images we present to them.
   D. Impressions of us are derived from:
      1. Facial expression, 55 percent.
      2. Voice tones, 37 percent.
      3. Words, 8 percent.
III. The Need for Listening
   A. We listen more than any other activity, except breathing.
   B. A manager spends up to 70 percent of the day communicating, at least 45 percent of the time managers are listening.
   C. Listening is a personal, human obligation.
   D. Without training, a listener retains only 25 percent of what he or she hears.
   E. Poor listening stems from bad habits.
   F. We can become good listeners. With training we can improve from 25 percent retention to nearly 50 percent retention.
   G. Making written or mental summaries of what we hear will lead to immediate listening improvement.

There you have an hour lecture highlighted in a logical, easy-to-read order.

Each listener should determine the best method to outline a talk. Studies by the Audio Visual Society show that trained notetakers are better listeners. Taking notes aids retention as well as comprehension. Where you can't take notes or the communication is brief, rely on mental summaries.

If you take notes, not only will you hear and understand better but you will have the data preserved for future use. However, the big bonus of it all is that you will be doing what is necessary to avoid the listening traps and distractions that you'll learn about in the next chapter.

Wherever you can, put the key ideas in writing. I'll explain mental outlines in greater detail in Chapter 6.

4
Stumbling Blocks to Active Listening

Were we as eloquent as angels,
yet we should please some men and some women
much more by listening than by talking.
> —Walter Colton

MAJOR BARRIERS AND COMMON PITFALLS

It is easy to overcome barriers and avoid pitfalls to listening once you are aware of what they are. Here are the major stumbling blocks to better listening.

Dan Daydreamer

First on the list of the worst listening habits is daydreaming as you are listening to a speaker. Meet Dan Daydreamer. You'll recognize him by his wandering eyes and turning head. Sometimes he will polish or clean his fingernails while someone is speaking to him. Or he will nervously tap a pencil, snap gum, drum his fingers, or just let his eyes and mind wander aimlessly. Daydreamers don't get the message, but they do lose friends. Don't be a Dan Daydreamer.

Freda Facts

Listening for facts only is another bad habit. Freda Facts will always have a mind full of little tidbits of truth, but she may be completely lost as to what the facts prove or what the speaker was trying to get across. Facts are important, of course, but more important is what they mean or what they add up to. In a court of law, for example, the facts are merely stepping stones, building blocks to prove a point. You'll learn more if you listen for ideas.

For example, I have stated the fact that most people use only about 25 percent of their native ability to listen. But *why* this is so is more important: the whys include bad habits and lack of training. Don't be a facts-only listener.

Stewart Slouch

Stewart Slouch makes good listening difficult if not impossible by slouching in his chair or over a table or counter as though he lacks vitamins or sleep. You can spot a good listener all the way across a room. The person's posture is alert, whether the listener is seated or standing, and the eyes and interest are concentrated on the speaker. An erect posture communicates interest, aliveness, and awareness. Remember, the biggest problem in communication is that we fail to focus on the other person's ideas. One big step toward improvement is an alert posture as we listen. Don't be a Stewart Slouch.

Finicky Fran

And don't be a Finicky Fran. Another barrier to total listening is calling the speaker or the subject uninteresting. The burden of listening and understanding is on the listener. Tuning out because we don't like the speaker's voice, hairdo, clothes, or topic is our problem. We may miss a golden opportunity for learning by not listening to what the speaker has to say because of looks or the fact the subject isn't one of our favorites.

We'll actually learn more from a topic that's unfamiliar to us. Reserve judgment until the speaker has finished. Don't waste time by tuning out. Try to learn from the speaker. As Ralph Waldo Emerson said, "Every person I meet is in some way my superior; that's what I learn from him or her."

Eddie Emotion

Eddie Emotion highlights another bad habit of listeners: He gets overly excited about things he hears. It might be because of a word he's misunderstood or because of a speaker's scowl, a screechy voice, or a shout. Whatever the cause of the emotion, it makes Eddie a poor listener. It's necessary to control emotion if you want to get the message and keep friends.

Temper tantrums or rash anger won't help communication at all. Keep your cool. Learn the reasons behind people's statements. Hear a person out completely, count to ten, bite your tongue gently, and don't be a poor listener by becoming an Eddie Emotion.

Remember the age-old saying "Sticks and stones will break my bones but names will never hurt me." Fighting and arguing accomplish nothing. They only waste our energy and rupture our relations with others. Resist the urge to overreact to charged words, such as *interest, taxes,* and *prices.* High emotions block listening. As Robert Frost remarked: "Education is the ability to listen to almost anything without losing your temper or your self-confidence."

Freddie Faker

Listening is a key to learning, yet many people are like Freddy Faker. They fake attention to the speaker, pretending to be getting the message. They smile, nod their heads, and even keep right on looking at the person who's speaking, but their minds have detoured and are probably involved in private planning.

Many students fake attention in school. It doesn't take any energy, whereas active listening is hard work and takes concentrated energy. These students are the ones who flunk or drop out because of lack of learning. Ask Freddy Faker a question and he is completely lost. He has to ask you, "What's the question?" because he was tuned out and didn't hear it.

People who fake attention are the losers. Sometimes they are so far off on a mental tangent you have to call their name two or three times to get them back to immediate consciousness. They were looking right at you, but the mind was miles away. There's power in rapt attention. Faking attention is a waste of time. Avoid the listening trap of becoming a Freddy Faker.

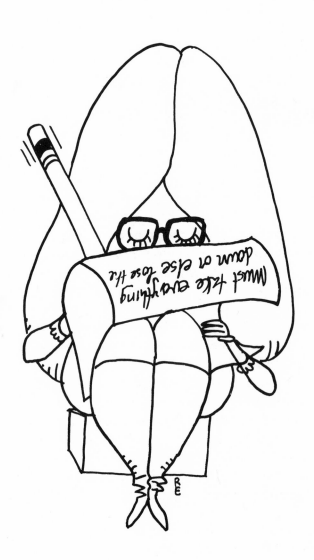

Nellie Notetaker

Now meet Nelly Notetaker. She tries to write down every word the speaker is saying. Even with shorthand, it would be difficult if not impossible to get the entire message down on paper, since most good platform speakers talk 150–200 words a minute. To hear and understand is practically impossible if you're trying to write down all or most of what you hear. In courses, workshops, seminars, and lectures I've conducted over the years, I've found that there are about five dedicated notetakers in every 100 listeners. And those five will be the only ones who complain I spoke too rapidly. If I were to slow down, the other 95 would complain I was too slow.

Good notetakers don't try to write down everything. They listen for highlights or key ideas and take more meaningful notes. Trying to write down all that you hear is the wrong way to listen because you miss the gestures, facial expressions, intent, and perhaps even what's said between the lines. Nelly Notetaker will miss the real message and be left with incomplete ideas. Make notes of *highlights* only.

Ted Timewaster

Ted Timewaster ignores the advantage of being able to listen faster than a person speaks. Instead of anticipating the points a speaker is making and mentally summarizing what is said, the Ted Timewasters of the world just sit and let the words go in one ear and out the other.

Unless you work at listening, you will fall into the bad habit of wasting the time you have to mentally anticipate, evaluate, and summarize as a person speaks. Identify the main ideas, and mentally summarize the essence of the communication. These are the positive steps that will keep you from becoming a Ted Timewaster. More on this in Chapters 5 and 6.

Don't let false notions keep you from improving your listening. Again, listening ability is not dependent on intelligence. Tests by the University of Minnesota have shown that people with high IQs are often terrible listeners, and many people with lower IQs test out superbly. It's a matter of good habits, training, desire, and concentration. A book like this or a course that teaches basic and advanced rules for better listening can provide you with the necessary knowledge.

Martha Mumbles

It would be wrong to say the fault is always in the listener when the communication is misunderstood. Only a small percentage of people have ever taken a speech course, so many people have poor speech habits. I call these habits hazardous to the listener and to a clear understanding of the message.

Speakers have equal responsibility for making sure their communication is heard and understood. Around 60 percent of misunderstanding in business has been traced to oral communication. You and I can help eliminate some of this by not becoming one of the seven sinister speakers who stifle effective listening.

First is Martha Mumbles. She swallows her words, and speaks too softly. Her voice trails off at the end of her sentences. She muffles her words.

SAN JOAQUIN DELTA COLLEGE LIBRARY

Roger Rambler

Next is Roger Rambler. He rambles on and on and on and on, never pausing for a reply. He never asks questions, just talks and talks. Any idea that comes up sends him off on a new tangent.

Roger specializes in one-way communication. His thoughts are illogical, his chatter aimless. Most people simply find him boring. Like the other sinister speakers in this section, Roger thwarts the human communications process at every turn.

Slow-Speaking Sally

Third is Slow-Speaking Sally. But look quickly because she'll put you to sleep with her monotonous tone. You'll be bored by anyone who speaks as slowly as Sally. Does she need vitamins, goals in life, or perhaps some fireworks to wake her up? In the old days, when a speaker was slow and dull, members of the audience would say, "Get a pitchfork and poke the speaker!" A 1979 Columbia University survey revealed that people do not trust the slow speaker.

Confidential Cal

Here comes Confidential Cal. Everything is so important or so secretive that Cal speaks in a low, confidential, guttural tone, not so much harsh as it is muffled. Many attorneys and insurance agents and some doctors fall victim to this habit. It takes energy to listen all right, but who needs the strain of trying to listen long to Confidential Cal? He needs to learn that it takes energy to speak up and be heard.

Nancy Nasal

Next in our unimpressive characters department is Nancy Nasal. She constantly talks through her nose. It's such an easy, lazy way of speaking. It doesn't take much effort at all. In fact, you hardly have to breathe when you talk through your nose. It's almost impossible for people to hear you when you have that nasal twang. Besides, it's irritating to the ears. But it's a dandy way to keep people from wanting to be around you.

Shifty-Eyed Sam

Here comes Shifty-Eyed Sam. Oh, he's honest, but his shifty eyes cause others to doubt his sincerity. His eyes are always darting around. A glance to the side, eyes following any movement or sound. People don't trust the shifty-eyed speaker or listener. This problem can curb business and friendships for the Sams of the world.

Hesitating Herb

Then there's Hesitating Herb. He's never sure of himself. He verges on a stutter many times. It could be caused by a lack of confidence in one's own ability or vocabulary, but it could also be a bad habit that gets worse with practice. People tend not to trust the person who hesitates while speaking. Besides, it's nerve wracking to try to listen for any length of time to such a speaker.

There you have seven additional characters high-lighting seven hazardous habits of speakers that frus-trate total listening. Work hard at avoiding these speaking habits. By doing so, you'll be helping others to understand you.

STAMP OUT DISTRACTIONS

Besides avoiding the worst listening traps or habits, we can do a great deal to minimize distractions when-ever we are engaged in conversation or listening to a speaker. Listening to someone over the telephone is included here. Keep your desk clear of articles, papers, and decorations. Always have a pad and pen or pencil handy, however. Try to remove or curtail any extraneous sounds from inside or outside the room. Many sounds from outside can be eliminated by closing doors and windows. Turn off any harsh music or sound seeping in through a loudspeaker.

You can also help other people listen when you're the speaker. Distortion often results from a poor microphone, worn loudspeakers, and even poor use of a microphone. Equipment should be checked out before an event. Make sure the volume is proper, not too loud or too low. Speak about five or six inches away from the mike, keep it at an angle and off to one side of your face. Don't talk straight into the micro-phone or you'll pop your Ps and Bs and distract your listeners.

Try to avoid playing with pencils or pens, paper clips, fingernails, a ring, your wristwatch, or the

BAD LISTENING HABITS TO AVOID

Daydreaming—Don't let your eyes wander or your head turn aimlessly about. Keep from drumming your fingers, snapping gum, or mindlessly handling pens, pencils, and so on.

Facts-only Listening—Facts are important but only as stepping stones of ideas leading to a major point. Don't keep your mind so occupied over minor tidbits that you miss the speaker's overall message.

Poor Posture—Poor posture communicates poor listening; so don't slouch. The good listener's posture is alert, with eyes and attention concentrated on the speaker, regardless of whether the listener is standing or seated.

Tuning Out—The burden of listening is on the listener. Don't automatically condemn a speaker or the subject as uninteresting; don't prejudice your listening because you don't like the speaker's looks, hairdo, voice, and so on.

Emotionalism—Whatever you're feeling about the speaker or his or her subject, hear the speaker out first. Don't allow yourself to become irritated or overstimulated by what is said or how it is said—otherwise, the message gets lost in the flash of emotions.

Faking Attention—Don't pretend to be getting the message while your mind has made a mental detour and is busy with completely different ideas. If the speaker tries to interract with you at this point, you'll find yourself completely lost.

Obsessive Note Taking—You can't try to write down all that a speaker is saying, word for word, and expect to hear the message. Just jot down the highlights or key ideas and pay more attention to hearing the message rather than to writing everything down.

Time Wasting—Don't waste your listening time. You can listen faster than the speaker can speak, so anticipate, evaluate, and mentally summarize the speaker's points as you listen.

change in your pocket as you talk or listen. All of these things distract and detract from the message and the speaker. Active, concentrated listening rules out playthings.

When you engage in important business talks, have someone outside the room answer your phone; put a hold on interruptions from others, such as drop-in guests, and even office business. You'll be able to give or get messages much more clearly and in much less time that way.

5
Basic Building Blocks for Total Listening

A good listener is not only
popular everywhere, but after a while
he knows something.
　　　　　　—Wilson Mizner

HERE ARE SIX basic guidelines for better listening. You can improve your listening the day you start practicing them. I'll cover some advanced techniques that will help assure close to a 100 percent improvement later on.

A stepladder has a number of rungs on it to help you move upward. I'm going to use the ladder idea to help you progress upward in the ability to be an active listener. I'm going to spell out L A D D E R with the six rules. This will make it easier to remember them.

THE EYES HAVE IT

First, the *L* stands for: Look at the other person. Look at the person who is talking to you. Also, always look at the person you're talking to. Looking directly at the person who is speaking shows dynamic interest. I don't mean staring at the other person, just looking into his or her eyes, but looking toward the person as he or she talks to you. You can look at the hairline, the neckline, watch the mouth as the person speaks, even notice the color of the eyes of the speaker.

But don't look at the floor or ceiling or out the window. And don't turn your eyes to view every distraction around you. People tell me they don't trust the person who doesn't look at them. They also sense suspicion, trickery, or distrust from such people. And distrust will block communication. It's a huge block also to motivation. There's little or no motivation when there is no respect. Concentrate on the other person as you listen. Looking at the person will enable you to judge the intent of the message as well as the content. So give your undivided attention as you listen to others. If you project genuine, active attention, you will convey sincere interest.

I was visiting a friend of mine who is also in the education field. She told her seven-year-old daughter to clean her room before dinner. At that moment, the child inquired, "Mommy, I wasn't looking when you said that. Did you say it with a smile or a frown?"

So, even first graders are already keenly aware of the importance of facial expression and body language. This seven-year-old wanted to know her mother's true intent. That is, did her mother really mean what she said? Likewise, you will know more when you observe the body language and facial expressions of others.

Again Rule 1, always look at the person you're talking to—and always look at the person who is talking to you. When the eyes are elsewhere, the mind is elsewhere.

THE ART OF ASKING QUESTIONS

Moving up the ladder to better listening, Rule 2 starts with *A*. Ask questions. This is the best way for anyone to become a better listener fast. It's a necessity for parents, teachers, managers, and salespeople. To keep from doing all the speaking yourself and to get the other person talking, develop the tools of the reporter, the art of asking questions. Master the different types of questions you'll learn now. Start using them today. Practice is the best instructor.

Some types of questions help you discover facts. You might want to know where someone works or lives, what they do, where they're from. Questions that get specific, concise facts for answers are called *closed-end questions*. You rarely get more than a word or two in reply. "What is your name?" is one example. "How old are you?" is another.

The opposite type is called *open-ended questioning*. You can find out most of the facts about a person by asking just one or two open-ended questions. For

67

SAN JOAQUIN DELTA COLLEGE LIBRARY

example, I might ask you, "How did you get into the line of work you're in now?" That question will usually get a person talking for at least 5 minutes and more likely for 15. Of course, you could simply say to someone, "Tell me about yourself." That's open-ended and will accomplish the same purpose.

Try to develop a skill for questioning others in conversation and in business communications. Naturally, you won't ask a lot of questions if you don't have the time and it isn't necessary. But when you have the time, try out these different types of questions and become accustomed to using them. We really don't take anything for our own without practice.

You might ask someone, "How did you get into the job you have now?", and even though it's an open-ended question, the person might simply answer, "By accident." Now what do you do? You ask a follow-up question, such as "What happened?" Then you'll get the person talking in depth.

We can learn a lesson from doctors, lawyers, and dentists on questioning skills. None of them would be able to help you unless they asked a few questions. Once the questions have been asked and the answers given, a lawyer may decide not to handle your case. Doctors and dentists can't help you at all until they find out what's wrong.

Doctors especially develop a skill for questioning. Perhaps psychiatrists, most of all, need the tools of questioning to help discover a patient's problem. Psychiatrists are paid $100 an hour and more to listen to

68

the problems of patients and try to help solve them. So in their training as therapists, they are taught to use skillful, open-ended questioning to get the whole story from a patient. Once the problem has been stated, the doctor might say, "That's interesting! Tell me more." Or "I don't understand. Could you give me an example?" This kind of questioning produces the answers needed to enable the doctor to help others.

First, ask fact-finding questions to discover what the problem is. Then, just as the medical doctor might, ask a question to discover how the person feels. People love to explain how they feel. Parents, managers, salespeople, anyone can learn more and get along better with other people by discovering how those people feel about things. Additional questions will also help gain an understanding of why they feel as they do.

I've often wondered how many sales are lost each week because the salesperson doesn't listen to the prospect or customer. There's been a revolution in selling. The change has taken us from the product-pusher of the past to the counselor-type salesperson who asks questions first. Contrary to the belief of many people, you actually save time and make the sale faster by asking the prospect some questions to discover his or her needs, problems, or objectives. I've conducted hundreds of role plays on videotape with salespeople over the years and have used a stopwatch to time their sales interview. I've discovered that it takes a shorter time to sell by using the questioning approach.

Besides, I've noted that the sale is almost always

made when questions are asked and the prospect participates. And the sale is rarely made when it's a one-way sellathon, with the salesperson spouting facts, features, benefits, and advantages without learning the definite needs or wants of the prospect.

People don't have time to listen to others rave on and on about their product or service in person or on the telephone. But they are willing to spend time with someone who is interested in their ideas, needs, and problems. Besides, it doesn't take long to find out what a person feels, needs, or wants.

To illustrate the power of questions, I think of the experience of a famous sales trainer and speaker, the late Fred Herman. Herman was introduced on the Mike Douglas television show one day as "the greatest salesman in the world." What happened next was purely spontaneous; Herman vowed he had no idea what Mike Douglas would ask him.

Douglas began by saying, "Fred, since you're hailed as the Number 1 salesman in the world, sell me something!" Without any hesitation, Fred Herman responded instantly and instinctively with a question: "Mike, what would you want me to sell you?"

Mike Douglas, who is paid a couple of million dollars a year for asking questions, was now on the defensive. Surprised, Douglas paused, looked around, and finally answered, "Well, sell me this ashtray."

Fred Herman again spoke instantly, "Why would you want to buy that?" And again, Mike Douglas, surprised and scratching his head, finally answered,

"Well, it's new and shapely. Also, it's colorful. And besides, we are in a new studio and don't want it to burn down. And, of course, we want to accommodate guests who smoke."

At this point, Mike Douglas sat back in his chair, but not for long. Instantly Fred Herman responded, "How much would you pay for the ashtray, Mike?"

Douglas stammered and said, "Well, I haven't bought an ashtray lately, but this one is attractive and large, so I guess I'd pay $18 or $20." And Fred Herman, after asking just three questions, closed the sale by saying, "Well, Mike, I'll let you have the ashtray for $18."

That's selling by questioning and listening. I call it selling with a professional ear. The whole sale took less than one minute. Fred Herman said he simply reacted as he always does in selling, by asking questions.

Follow the method of professional listeners. Learn to ask questions and develop a big ear for listening.

Rudyard Kipling, the famous author, summed up the skill of questioning in these words: "I have six honest servants. They've taught me all I know. Their names are who, what, where, when, why and how."

You'll find that who, where, and when are opening words for closed-end questions that produce monosyllabic replies. Whereas, what, why, and how generally begin open-ended questions and produce much more detailed information.

Practice Rule 2 every day. Make it your personal

goal to ask a lot of questions. But have a purpose for each question. There are two basic categories: to get specific information or to learn opinions and feelings. It's easier to gain a rapport and get a person to open up by relating your questions to the other person's background or experience. Use open-ended questions to draw out. Remember, closed-end questions will make it difficult to get another person to speak and share ideas or information. Nobody likes to feel they're being investigated.

Finally, remember the advice of the famous statesman of some years ago Bernard Baruch, who said: "You can win more friends in two months by showing interest in others than you can in two years by trying to interest others in you." Looking at people as you converse with them and asking questions will help show genuine interest.

Don't Interrupt

Continuing up the ladder of success in listening, Rule 3 is the first of the two *D*'s: **Don't** interrupt. It's just as rude to step on people's ideas as to step on their toes.

It's a human tendency to want to jump right into a conversation when we get an idea or are reminded of something by someone's words. And that's why there's a problem. We need to continually practice letting other people finish their sentences or ideas. Speak only in turn is the answer.

Most of us avoid interrupters. We even go out of our

way to avoid them. In fact, a desire to prevent interruptions motivated Thomas Jefferson to invent the dumbwaiter, a mechanical lift to take food and drink by pulley from the kitchen to an upstairs dining room. Jefferson disliked being interrupted in conversation by servants; with the dumbwaiter, no servants were necessary and he couldn't be interrupted.

Nobody likes to be cut off while speaking. So work at letting others finish what they have to say. Bite your tongue and count to 10 if you have to, but practice Rule 3.

Don't Change the Subject

Rule 4 for better listening is the second *D*: **D**on't change the subject. This is a little different from Rule 3. Interrupting is bad enough, but going right on and changing the subject at the same time is positively rude. Some people do this so much they are dodged by others who don't want to be their next victim.

Consider a group of people who are talking and one of the members says, "I was watching television the other night and Senator Hayakawa of California spoke about. . . ." Now at this point, another member of the group, hearing the word *California*, interrupts immediately and changes the subject. "Oh, California, have you been out there to Disneyland? It's terrific! We took the kids there last summer and had a ball. You know, they have an island there, Tom Sawyer Island. And they have tree-houses, caves, all kinds of things to do. Why, you could spend a couple of days there.

You get to the island on a raft or on one of those old Mississippi steamboats. Boy, it was just like being Robinson Crusoe on that island. Now what were you saying?"

Well, the speaker who was going to say something about Senator Hayakawa of California has no doubt buried that idea forever. In fact, the person who was cut off will not offer any more ideas and will probably find a reason to get out of the presence of the interrupter who also changed the subject.

Interrupting and changing the subject are sure ways to alienate people quickly. So try to curb both tendencies. You can be certain of this: If you cut people off while they're speaking and also change the subject, you'll be cutting them out of your life as friends or associates as well. A little restraint will pay big dividends.

CHECK YOUR EMOTIONS

Going on up the ladder to success in listening, our next rung is the letter E, for Emotions. Rule 5 is to check your emotions. Some people are prone to anger and get excited about certain words.

It doesn't pay to get overstimulated and overreact to the words and ideas of others. Words such as gasoline, taxes, 7 percent, abortion, and communism can stir one's emotions instantly. Curb your emotions. Control your urge to interrupt and stifle the other person's idea. It's a free country. People are entitled to their opinions and the right to complete their thoughts. Hear others out.

74

Let others explain their points of view, ideas, or convictions. Cutting them off won't accomplish anything. Try to understand them first. Then give your own ideas in a controlled manner. Little is gained through arguing and fighting. On the contrary, usually loss of time and injured relationships result.

Evaluate when the idea is complete, not before, or only when you fully understand the other person's meaning. I'll cover evaluation more fully when I discuss the advanced principles of listening.

I know a fellow who went storming into his boss's office. He was shouting and complaining that someone not as long with the company had received a promotion he thought he should have gotten. The boss told him that because of his quick temper he couldn't be trusted to manage others.

Besides, getting overly excited causes us to mentally debate or fight any idea that differs from our personal conviction, experience, or bias. So we don't hear what the speaker is saying at these times. Remember, the biggest problem in listening is failing to concentrate on the other person's communication. Getting overly emotional about something is one of the causes of the problem. Following the LADDER will help us avoid the pitfalls of poor listening. Check your emotions. Hear the other person out first.

LISTEN RESPONSIVELY

Finally, the top rung of the ladder. The *R* stands for an essential principle of better listening and therefore better understanding: **R**esponsiveness. Be a responsive listener. Be responsive in your demeanor, posture, and facial expression. Let your whole being show you are interested in other people and their ideas.

As you listen, look at the other person and show some signs of hearing and understanding. Nod your head occasionally—gently, not vigorously. Nod slightly with a yes for agreement or a no when it's something sad or unhappy. Show through your posture, whether seated or standing, that you are concentrating on listening totally.

We show our interest in others also when we say occasionally "Um-mm" or "Uh-huh." These simple signs encourage speakers. They show we're interested in them and that we're listening to what they're saying. However, others won't talk long unless we are responsive in our listening and offer some nonverbal and even some slight verbal signs of understanding.

To understand this important principle of being responsive, it helps to ask, "How do we turn people off?" The answers come quickly: by not looking at them, not asking questions, not showing any positive response; by looking at our watch or out the window, shuffling papers, interrupting, and giving other negative types of feedback.

But we want to turn people on, not off. Whether we're teachers, managers, doctors, parents, or salespeople, we want to encourage others to communicate with us so we can gain understanding.

And there's one more important part to being responsive in listening to others: The one time it is all right, even desirable, to interrupt is to clarify what is said. For example, as soon as you hear someone's name when you are introduced, inquire right at that moment how to spell the name if it is a difficult one. Or if you aren't sure of a statistic, date, place, or other fact someone mentions, it shows responsive, concentrated listening to interrupt to clarify.

You can cushion your interruption with "Pardon me." But sometimes that isn't necessary. You might simply inquire "How many?" or "When did it happen?" or "What's the name?" The interruption to clarify will actually help you focus on the other person's message more actively.

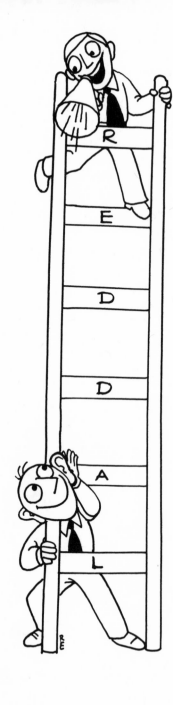

Responsively listen.

Express emotion with control.

Don't change the subject.

Don't interrupt.

Ask questions.

Look at the other person.

Use the Ladder to Successful Listening

All six rungs of the LADDER are positive steps that will help you concentrate on the person who is speaking. The six rules of successful listening are shown on the opposite page. Practice the rules every day in conversations with people. Before you know it, you'll be using them naturally and without self-consciousness. And friends and associates will soon be complimenting you on your ability to listen totally to others.

6
Advanced Principles for Total Listening

*Talk to a man about himself
and he will listen for hours.*
—Benjamin Disraeli

WE'VE COVERED the negative habits and barriers to listening, and we've built a stepladder of six basic rules to encourage communication and foster effective listening. Now it's important to learn some advanced rules that help ensure understanding and recall. There are four major advanced principles. You can remember these four principles easily with the one word: HEAR.

The *H* stands for: **H**ave a hearing checkup from an ear specialist. Our hearing is too precious to take it for granted. It will be difficult to listen totally if our hearing is less than normal.

The *E* stands for: **E**valuate the evidence the speaker offers to support his or her ideas.

The *A* stands for: **A**nticipate the point of the communication, the meaning of the message.

And the *R* stands for: **R**eview mentally the key points or ideas of the speaker. Mentally summarize the essence of the message you're hearing. This is the most important of all the basic and advanced rules for better listening; practiced faithfully, it is the rule that can contribute most to doubling your listening powers.

Using these four principles will guarantee the elimination of most of the bad habits and pitfalls covered in Chapter 2. Let's examine the principles in depth one at a time.

HAVE A HEARING CHECKUP

Comedian Henny Youngman uses this one-liner: "Got hearing trouble? Hang a wire from your ear and most people will automatically talk louder!" True as that may be, it would be best to get your hearing tested to make sure that your hearing is OK. Many people have partial hearing loss, but they never take the trouble to find out; they are forever asking people to repeat themselves. Another usual indication of poor hearing is when a person is always shouting, even in one-to-one conversation.

Unfortunately, 33 million Americans have a significant hearing impairment, and the number is rising all the time. People usually associate poor hearing with old age, yet 27 million of the 33 million Americans with hearing deficiency are under age 65.

Experts point out that hearing loss can occur at any age, in any degree, to either sex and completely apart from other physical or biological deficiencies. Noise is an increasing source of ear damage in our environment. In many cases, people with faulty hearing are confused, frustrated, or even frightened about what has happened, why it has happened, and what to do about it.

An excellent book is available for an in-depth study of hearing: *Our Endangered Hearing—Understanding and Coping with Hearing Loss* by Richard Carmen.* This book offers a frank, fresh look at hearing loss. It dispels the myths and misconceptions and describes the mechanics of hearing, the anatomical structures involved, types of hearing loss, and treatment available for specific conditions. Carmen completes his book with a series of questions and answers and case studies that provide practical information for people who have hearing impairments.

It is sad that society leans toward outmoded ideas about hearing loss or ideas based on rumors, superstitions, and falsehoods. So my first suggestion to you for improved listening is, if you have the slightest suspicion that you have a hearing problem, see an ear

*Emmaus, Pa.: Rodale Press, 1980. (Carmen is the audiologist for Southern California Permanent Medical Group and editor of *Hear,* a publication by the Southern California Hearing Council.)

specialist and get a hearing test. A whole new world could open up to you once any deficiency is corrected. It's worth the cost of the examination to discover any hearing impediment. Hearing aids are better today, and they are smaller, hardly even detectable. Hearing is a golden gift, just as sight is. But the ear has the ability to pick up sounds in a 360° circumference, whereas the eye at best takes in just 180° degrees. The ear is sharp, too. If you close your eyes and have someone walk to different parts of a large room or auditorium, you can point to where the sound is coming from with 100 percent accuracy every time.

Once you've had any hearing problems corrected, you're ready to tackle other distractions, distortions, and negative traits. I think it's important to stress once again the necessity for a person to have a desire to listen actively. This is also called concentrated listening. It takes self-control to avoid distractions that bombard us almost everywhere we go. The nineteenth-century clergyman Henry Ward Beecher summed it up in one sentence: "One hour of intense concentration will accomplish more than years of dreaming."

EVALUATE THE EVIDENCE

E is for the principle that every courtroom case is required to follow. Evaluate the supporting evidence the speaker offers. Evidence comes in many forms: statistics, analogies, exhibits, demonstrations, and testimonials, perhaps with such visual aids as photographs, maps, charts, graphs, and slides.

The Romans had a saying about evidence: "Any talk without a specific example is weak." So ask yourself as you listen to a speaker, "Am I getting definite evidence or just generalities?" "Is the talk factual or strictly opinions?" "What is the speaker's point?" "What is the speaker trying to prove?" The truest test of evidence is whether the speaker is specific or not. Are you getting answers to the reporter's questions: who, what, where, when, why, and, perhaps, how?

Listening for facts only is a poor listening habit. Listening for what the facts prove, what they add up to is better. Listen for ideas, concepts, specific points.

For example, if I'm giving a stirring speech about how George Washington and the men at Valley Forge persistently engaged in battle in spite of freezing cold, snow, and ice, I'm trying to make a point about being persistent and never giving up. However, if I happen to mention they had horses at Valley Forge and George Washington had a horse named Stanley, those are facts.

You go home after the talk and your spouse asks, "How was the talk? What did you learn?" And you answer, "Honey, did you know George Washington had a horse named Stanley?" And your spouse replies, "So what? What was the point of the talk?" And then you answer, "I don't know."

You see, it's easy to get interested in facts and miss the message. Again, the point was "Never give up! Be persistent!" Many professors and trainers build in some catchy facts or phrases to test if people are hearing what's being said. Sometimes people keep right on taking notes when the facts might not even be true.

The George Washington incident is used by Herb True, a professional speaker, to make a similar point about the proper way to listen. A second illustration he incorporates into his lectures is a method of discovering if executives are really hearing and understanding what is being said.

If the listeners are taking notes furiously, they may not be absorbing the meaning of his points. So, at a midpoint of a presentation, True will say, "Along these same lines, psychologists note that if your parents didn't have children, it's likely you won't have children." If the audience members keep writing and don't offer a chuckle in response, True calls for a break. The members are not really listening.

As you evaluate the evidence, the supporting data for a speaker's points, watch the facial expressions, posture, and gestures. (I'll have much more to say about the impact of body language in communication in Chapter 7.) And listen between the lines for what isn't said, so you can learn what is indicated though not spoken. For example, I heard a man and a wife both speak on a program one time. From the things they said it was possible to know how old each one was and how long they had been married. They didn't mention the information specifically, but by listening between the lines you could deduce the facts.

A word, an idea, testimony, or evidence cannot always be understood without questioning. A word has no meaning unless we agree on what it means. For 500 common words used every day, the dictionary gives over 14,000 meanings. It takes feedback, checking, or clarification by questioning to assure understanding.

A friend of mine called one night on the phone and said, "Bob, how about coming over?" I said, "OK!" Two hours later I called him and said, "I thought you were coming over?" He replied, "I meant how about you coming over here." Often the simplest communication is misunderstood because we don't take time to check for feedback and make sure we have the same understanding. Voltaire put it in these words: "If you want to discourse with me, define your terms."

The New York *Post* carried a brief item a year or so after the death of J. Edgar Hoover, former director of the FBI. The story can be summarized this way: When Hoover, reviewing a lengthy report, became annoyed because the writer had not respected the margin requirements, the director scribbled at the top of the first page, "Watch the borders." The report went its rounds. No one understood, but no one dared ask. So orders went out to the FBI field offices to "watch the borders." For several weeks agents stood guard along the Mexican and Canadian borders.

Imagine how much money that one misunderstanding cost you and me. If only one person had asked the director what he meant. Perhaps the director should have been more precise by writing, "Watch the margins." The same sort of misunderstanding is common in oral business communications every day because nobody checks to clarify the information. Just a question or two can make sure we understand clearly and establish the authenticity of the evidence.

In the news a while back there was a story about the Consolidated Edison Power Company of New York that was headlined: "If Only Con Ed Listened." The story in brief said, that the blackout of New York City in July 1977 could have been averted if Con Ed had not ignored a warning from the State Power Pool to cut its power just 32 minutes before the lights went out.

On a tape recording, the State Power Pool spokesman said, "You better get rid of some load." And a Con Edison worker replied, "You're right, you're right!" But even though that conversation occurred at 9:02 P.M., the lights went out all over New York City at 9:34 P.M. So evidently listening is not enough; evaluating the evidence or the situation is also imperative. Then of course, as at Con Edison, action is often necessary once the impact of the message is understood.

Sometimes the truth is hard to understand and it takes concentrated, even concerned listening to identify it. Many centuries ago, Buddha told a story you may be familiar with. It highlights our need for, as well as the difficulty of, corroborating evidence and getting at the truth.

The story is about the blind men and the elephant. The blind men were taken to examine the elephant. Taking hold of the tail, one of them began to swing back and forth on it. He said, "The elephant is like a rope." Another blind man got hold of the trunk and curled it up. He remarked, "The elephant is like a serpent." Another of the blind men took hold of the elephant's leg. He observed, "The elephant is like a tree." A fourth touched the side of the elephant and said, "The elephant is like a house." Another blind man, taking hold of the elephant's ear, remarked, "Why, the elephant is like a fan." Every one of the blind men spoke a truth, a fact. But all the individual facts still didn't describe the elephant.

I attended a meeting recently at a midtown New York hotel. The speaker represented one of the daily newspapers. He gave a fine talk. When the meeting ended I approached the speaker to clarify a fact. I asked him, "Did you say a Dr. Paul Green at the University of Chicago made the statement 'If you learn to solve problems, you can add five years to your life?' " I loved the quotation and wanted to use it in teaching conference leadership and for conducting conferences on problem solving.

The speaker replied, "Oh, I just made that up about the university affiliation. I don't know where he is."

Wanting to evaluate the evidence even more, I asked, "Why did you make up a university affiliation at all?" The speaker answered, "Well, I felt that would give the statement greater authenticity."

It's wise to verify what people say. I heard a member of an audience challenge a professional speaker one time by asking, "Why is it that all of your

*Have a
hearing checkup.*

*Evaluate
the evidence.*

*Anticipate
key points.*

*Review
mentally.*

statistics end with a fraction?" The speaker replied, "Because people are more likely to believe them." He lost my trust at that moment by admitting the figures weren't accurate.

With people who are trying to convince us with falsehoods, you can see how important it is to seek corroboration of statistics, statements, facts, quotations, and other evidence. Ask "Who said it? When? Where? Can I see it? What magazine or book?" Don't accept the greatest liar of all, "They say. . . ." Don't accept someone saying "a recent survey." Ask "What survey? Who made it? When was it made? Where can I see it?"

Unfortunately, a lot of people make up things they say. Because some of these people are involved in selling, many states in the last few years have passed laws requiring salespeople to state that the contract can be canceled up to three days after the day it is signed.

In the past, a door-to-door salesperson would get a down payment for a product or service and never be seen again. The unsuspecting prospect failed to evaluate the evidence. Ask for the salesperson's card with the address and phone number of the company. Ask for testimonials of satisfactory service given to others, perhaps even in your neighborhood. Then check out the phone number and address. Call a satisfied customer. Good salespeople will welcome the checkup. And you could save yourself time and money.

Now let's summarize this second advanced principle of better listening: evaluate. Ask questions to be sure you understand the message you hear and to identify the source of surveys, statistics, testimonials, quotations, or other data. There can be no gullibility in effective leadership. Don't be deceived.

Follow this principle faithfully to get at the truth, to avoid spreading false gossip, and to learn by being analytical and inquisitive. If you do, you'll be a wiser person and a better leader, and you'll avoid being the victim of false or incorrect information. Consider the fellow who rushed up to a friend of his and said, "Hi Bill! Congratulations!" Bill replied, "What for?" And the man answered, "For making $50,000 in oil." Bill admonished the friend, "It wasn't I, it was my brother. It wasn't oil, it was coal. And he didn't *make* $50,000, he lost it." "Well," said the friend, "I was approximately correct."

ANTICIPATE KEY POINTS OR IDEAS

The third of the four advanced principles is to anticipate what the speaker is leading to, what point will be made. Anticipating is a natural trait of the human mind in listening or reading. Most people have seen mystery movies and have read mystery books. In a Sherlock Holmes book or movie, a great deal of the excitement is to anticipate the outcome of the story. This is true in almost any novel, and it's even true in the soap operas on television. But it's especially common to try to guess the outcome of a murder mystery. That's why they're called whodunits. We try to outwit the writer and guess who committed the crime. Sometimes we're right and sometimes we're wrong. But in either case, anticipation heightens the excitement of the mystery, and it makes our listening more effective and more enjoyable as well.

When you anticipate what point the speaker will make or what the evidence adds up to, you win no matter what happens. First, if you anticipate correctly, you have the point well ahead. This assures correct understanding and even gives you lead time, since you know the conclusion in advance. Second, if you anticipate the wrong point, a different one, you still win because you can apply a key principle of education: compare and contrast.

Besides, in order to anticipate what point the speaker will make, you will have to concentrate on the content and avoid a dozen or more traps or barriers to good listening. So you can't lose by anticipating what a speaker is leading to. Again, even if it's a surprise ending, you'll understand the communication better.

Still, many people feel it's a hindrance to anticipate. Perhaps a little practice will help. Also, I didn't say anticipate so far ahead or so far off the beam you lose track of what the speaker is saying. Simply listen as the person speaks, but try to foresee what point might be made. It's an excellent technique just to keep us focusing on the message of the other person.

But there's another reason this principle is an excellent one, and this is an important fact for listeners, speakers, and learners of any kind. The average person speaks at about 125 words per minute in person-to-person conversation and about 100 words per minute to an audience, but the average person can hear up to 400 words a minute. Above-average people—many managers, executives, and well-educated people—can listen six to eight times as fast as the average person speaks. This means that the above-average person can hear and assimilate 600–800 words a minute. So there's plenty of time for the listener to anticipate and absorb what the speaker is saying.

Professional speakers and teachers know about this thought–speech speed differential. They know that if they don't speak rapidly, at far more than 100–125 words per minute, they will bore the audience in five minutes or less. All the top platform speakers who are paid $1,000 or more for an hour speech know this, and most of them talk at an average of 200 words per minute. But even at this rate, listeners still have time to anticipate.

Top speakers have good content and vitality, but the key common quality that makes them in demand is summed up in one word: *pace,* the art of speaking faster and slower. The pros know it is essential to speed up on less consequential data and to slow down on the technical, complex, or statistical material or to make important points. This is what I teach the hundreds of speakers and teachers I train each year around the world, that pace is a key difference between the amateur and the professional style of delivery. Of course, vitality is a prerequisite or they wouldn't be able to display the kind of pace I'm talking about.

About 5 people out of 100 will feel you're speaking too fast. But if you slow down, the 95 others will call you boring. These are my figures from years of study and years of being evaluated after talks. The five who say it's too fast usually have a problem. Often, they're people who listen for facts only. Or they're hard of hearing, poor notetakers, or too analytical.

Some people want to write down everything they hear. This is a mistake. They miss the meaning of the message for one thing. Besides, it's darn near impossible to write down everything a good speaker is saying because of the fast pace. The best way to take notes is to listen for what's new, what's different, what you hadn't thought of before, and to write down just the highlights. Don't listen for facts only; listen for the ideas that the facts prove.

I mention these things to help you learn additional insights for perfecting your hearing and listening ability. And I feel the knowledge of the thought–speech differential will help you improve even faster.

To summarize the third of the three principles in our aim to be a better listener: You've plenty of mental time to anticipate the ideas of most people you hear, and you will avoid the listening traps of detouring, daydreaming, mentally debating, private planning, and a dozen other common pitfalls of poor listening. Again, if you anticipate, you'll find it almost impossible to get off the subject you're hearing.

Don't forget, if you're right, you have the point ahead of time. If you're wrong, you can compare your point with the speaker's point; you learn by comparison and contrast.

REVIEW MENTALLY

Next, the fourth advanced principle in our aim to be a better listener: Review what the speaker says; mentally summarize what you hear. It's the most important rule of all for listening improvement. In fact, it's the one indispensable principle. By following it faithfully, you can improve your listening 100 percent.

Do a little mental review every couple of minutes in longer talks, tapes, sermons, or speeches. For shorter conversations, talks, or reports, a couple of mental minisummaries will assure you of remembering the essence of the communication.

A review or mental summary often involves no more than simply asking yourself questions as you're listening to a speaker. Remember, you have plenty of time to do this, since you can hear four to eight times faster than most speakers speak. And you will understand the message better and retain it longer by mentally summarizing what you hear.

IBM Corporation has a one-word motto: THINK. The word is printed in every major language on small cards that are put on training desks in IBM classrooms. To think as you focus on what someone is saying to you is the key to listening improvement. If you think as you listen, it will be easy to mentally outline what you are learning. Ask yourself, "What point is this speaker making? What are the key ideas here?"

Try to summarize the essence of the message, the overall communication, not just the facts. Try to highlight the point or key points of the talk. Maybe you'll ask yourself "What's the problem here?" or "What is it this speaker wants me to do?" Questions help you follow the message.

Making mental minireviews is the quick, effective way to improve your listening. Again, this habit is easy to acquire with a little practice. Try reviewing whatever others say in conversation.

Another benefit of mental review is that you will avoid such listening traps as faking attention or taking mental detours. Doing mental reviews of what you're hearing will keep you concentrating on the essence of the communication.

I've purposely used the acronyms LADDER and HEAR to organize my basic and advanced rules for total listening to make it easy for you to summarize and remember the main points. You can double your chances of understanding and retaining the theme of formal speech or informal conversation with occasional mental summaries. But it does take some practice to get accustomed to always reviewing what you hear.

Once you've acquired the ability and it becomes second nature, you will no longer forget names and facts when you hear them. The mental questioning and reviewing you do will almost guarantee understanding and retention. A desire to improve and concentration are prerequisites for good listening and a good memory. Honest listening takes concentration.

In most endeavors, people will be effective to the degree they are able to concentrate. To develop your concentration powers, avoid everything that might distract you. Keep meetings private. No phones ringing, no knocks on the door. Keep your desk, briefcase, and even your pockets from being overloaded. Order and organization foster concentration. It's a matter of self-control that improves with practice.

Hearing is one thing. Conscious listening is another. Some call it concerned listening. This means that we make a conscious effort to follow what is being said and a sincere effort to understand it. We are actually being selective in our listening. We are trying to get the point of the communication. In longer talks we want to discover the center of interest.

When we receive instructions or hear an announcement, we should listen for details that answer the questions what, when, where, who, how, and why? For lectures, reports, and speeches, we should be listening for the main ideas and the central theme or concept. We should listen from the beginning and with an open mind. Someone once observed that the mind is like a parachute: It doesn't work unless it's open.

It's necessary to listen for the supporting details and relate them to the main theme. It's also important not to let bias, prejudices, or dislike of a speaker's looks, voice, or manner distract us. Distractions make it almost impossible to hear with understanding, because distractions prevent effective mental reviews.

In any kind of listening—analytical, appreciative, or instructional—it takes real effort to avoid physical and mental distractions and concentrate on the speaker and the message. And it takes self-control to organize the ideas as you hear them. Mental reviews are no more than a means of identifying and organizing key ideas. Sometimes that takes intelligent mental questioning, if you're listening to a speech, and actual questions to clarify, if you are engaged in person-to-person conversation or in a meeting.

The responsibility for learning is on the listener. As the English journalist and author G. K. Chesterton said years ago, "In all the world, there's no such thing as an uninteresting subject; there are only uninterested people." Doing the work required for mentally summarizing what you're hearing is the key, but don't overlook listening between the lines, noting the facial expressions, posture, and vocal tones of the speaker. Your review will be more accurate and more complete if you're a keen observer as you are listening. (See Chapter 7.)

What do you think was the problem of the listeners in this old story I'm going to relate to you? See if you feel it was lack of concentration, not reading between the lines, calling the speaker uninteresting, or all three.

The Irish dramatist Lord Dunsany, in one of his

plays, tells how the king called the prophet into his court. The king and his wives were present. The prophet stood up and in a loud voice said, "There was a king, and the king had soldiers to fight for him. He had slaves to work for him and hate him. And the number of slaves who worked for him and hated him was greater than the number of soldiers who fought for him and died for him, and the days of that king were few."

One of the queens said, "What a strange voice." Another queen said, "I don't like the cut of his garment." Although they had ears, they heard not, and the days of that king *were* few.

To effectively review what we're listening to, we must *hear* it clearly and understand it. The king and his wives weren't getting the message at all. You hear the message by listening attentively and even sensitively.

In short, listening selectively is the beginning of our work; doing mental summaries is next. Sometimes this is difficult because many speakers don't have a purpose or an outline. They talk in generalities, and they don't ever make a point. But if you and I are doing the work of evaluating the content and of organizing and reviewing the ideas, we will profit from every speech we hear and we will recognize the unprepared speaker.

Always listen with a receptive attitude. Also, listen empathically. Empathic listening is sensitive listening, trying to put yourself in the other person's shoes.

Half listening is like racing your car's engine with the gears in neutral. You use gas, but you get nowhere. So start today to always concentrate wholeheartedly on understanding every person you listen to, and really *hear*.

Aim to be a superior listener, to listen totally to others. And remember the most important rule of all, review mentally the main idea or the key points of every communication you hear. If you do, you'll surprise yourself and others at your new skill in listening.

7
Listening
Between the Lines

What you are speaks so loudly,
I can't hear what you say.
      —Ralph Waldo Emerson

UNDERSTANDING BODY LANGUAGE

Sigmund Freud noted in 1905 the significance of body language in understanding totally what people mean, think, and feel. Freud said, "No mortal can keep a secret. If his lips are silent, he chatters with his fingertips; betrayal oozes out of every pore!" It helps to listen with your eyes as well as your ears.

These days, books, magazine articles, and courses in body language abound. The main idea experts proclaim is that it takes a cluster of two or three body movements or positions to indicate a valid conclusion. Judging from just one movement or position could easily lead to a false assumption.

Someone listening to a speech might have his chin resting in his palm. You might think this reveals that the person is disbelieving, belligerent, or bored. But that's doubtful. Just one body position could mean any one of a dozen things, and it might have no meaning at all. For example, the chin resting in the hand may simply be the most comfortable position, or the person might be tired or maybe have a toothache.

But when there's a cluster of nonverbal actions, the message becomes quite clear. For instance, someone comes into your office to see you about something. You tell the person you always have an open door and plenty of time to help. But as you say that you have time, you are tapping your fingers and your foot while simultaneously looking at your wristwatch. There's a cluster of three actions that says to someone who can read between the lines that you are not ready to listen with open ears or an open mind at this time. You are preoccupied and would prefer not to be interrupted.

Oh, as you drum your fingers on the desk, the dreamer might think, "Boy, what a fine Latin beat!" But the realist says, "This is evidently a bad time to see him. He's not ready or willing to hear me now. I'll come back later."

The study of body language is not new, as Freud's observation indicates. Many people communicate an attitude that differs from what they say by their example, character, or actions. Edgar Guest, the poet, wrote, "I'd rather see a sermon any day than hear one." Aristotle said, "Character is the most effective agent of persuasion." So it's more than just what we say that communicates to people.

Everything by which you and I extend ourselves is communication: the way we talk and walk; our handshake, handwriting, facial expressions, voice, gestures. Even our birth sign communicates something to those who study astrology. We judge people by what they say and how they say it, what they do and how they do it, and what they think and why they think it.

A childhood jingle indicates how we sometimes prejudge people by what we see. It goes like this:

> I do not like thee, Dr. Fell.
> The reason why I cannot tell.
> But this I know and know full well:
> I do not like thee, Dr. Fell.

A story with a similar message is told about Charles Lamb. When he was walking down the street with a companion one day, Lamb suddenly said, "I can't stand that man across the street." His companion replied, "I didn't know you knew him." Lamb responded, "Of course I don't know him. If I knew him, I couldn't dislike him."

Questioning others and getting to know them will help establish a good mutual relationship. But listening between the lines, reading facial expression, body movement, and tone of voice will help you know and understand any person much better. When you keenly observe body movements, you'll be listening between the lines and you'll learn the intent as well as the content of the message.

In the Bible, a line in Proverbs reads, "The purpose in a person's mind is like deep water; but an individual of understanding can draw it out." Often the voice, facial expressions, gestures, or body movements and positions will reveal much more than words.

The human voice is so revealing that I could say to a person "I despise you," yet be seductive. So listen critically to people's vocal tones and emphasis to fully understand their communications. For example, the meaning of any sentence changes depending on which word is emphasized. Here's a sentence with six words that has six different meanings depending on which word is emphasized: (1) *I* never said he stole money; (2) I *never* said he stole money; (3) I never *said* he stole money; (4) I never said *he* stole money; (5) I never said he *stole* money; and (6) I never said he stole *money*.

Did you realize how the emphasis of just one word can change the meaning of a sentence so completely? It's as dramatic a difference as putting a drop of ink in a glass of water. The single drop changes the color of the entire glass of water. Pay closer attention to what is revealed in people's voices, by their tone, emphasis, pitch, force, and pace. The message could be in *how* they say something rather than in *what* they say.

Listening between the lines to understand someone's body language is a skill that comes with knowl-

106

edge and practice. It requires a course in itself. Body movements might be revealing much more than the average person realizes.

The late Theodore Reik, a protégé of Sigmund Freud, held the view that an essential interaction between the analyst and the patient takes place in psychoanalysis. He called this "listening with the third ear." Reik said that the analyst, by using creative intuition—the "third ear"—can sense the unspoken and unconscious thoughts of his patients and employ them to therapeutic effect.

TELLTALE SIGNALS

Now I'll present a few ideas about what to watch for as clues to a person's true thinking or feelings as they talk to you. And remember, it takes a cluster of two or more movements or gestures to indicate a true attitude or feeling.

Open hands and an unbuttoned coat indicate an openness about a person. On the other hand, defensiveness is indicated by arms crossed over the chest, crossed legs, an index finger pointed at others while talking, karate chops, and fistlike gestures. Hands on the hips is also a defensive gesture. Crossing the arms glancing sideways, touching or rubbing the nose, rubbing the eyes, buttoning the coat, and drawing away indicate suspicion.

Cooperation is shown by open hands, sitting on the edge of the chair, unbuttoning the coat, tilting the head, and hand-to-face gestures.

Frustration can be noted in speakers or listeners who breathe or speak in short breaths, wring their hands, rub the back of their neck, rub their hands through their hair, or use fistlike gestures or point the index finger.

You indicate insecurity when you pinch your flesh, chew a pen or pencil, rub one thumb over another, bite your fingernails, or keep your hands in your pockets.

Nervousness is shown openly by clearing your throat, smoking, whistling, covering your mouth with your hand as you speak, tugging at your pants while seated, jingling money in you pockets, tugging at your ear, wringing your hands, fidgeting in your chair, picking or pinching your flesh, and not looking at the other person.

You show confidence when you have your hands in your coat pockets with the thumbs out or on the lapels of your coat, sit up straight, steeple your hands, or have your hands behind your back.

One final category of body movements shows you are thinking things over or judging the matter: stroking your chin, tilting you head, hand-to-face gestures, peering over your glasses, taking your glasses off or cleaning them, pipe smoker gestures, biting on the earpiece of your glasses, and putting your hand to the bridge of your nose.

Observing facial expressions will be remarkably dependable in determining a person's feelings. A smile, a frown, a puzzling look are just a few of the expressions that communicate such feelings as fear,

Some Attitudes Communicated Through Body Language

Cooperation
Upper body in sprinter's position
Open hands
Sitting on edge of chair
Hand-to-face gestures
Unbuttoning of coat

Insecurity
Flesh pinching
Chewed pen, pencil
Thumb over thumb
Fingernail biting
Hands in pockets

Frustration
Short breaths
"Tsk" sound
Tightly clenched hands
Hand wringing
Pointing of index finger
Hand "combing" hair

Defensiveness
   Arms crossed on chest
   Legs crossed
   Fistlike gestures
   Pointing of index finger

Confidence
   Steepled hands
   Hands behind back
   Back stiffened
   Hands on coat lapels

Openness
   Open hands
   Unbuttoned coat

Evaluation
　　Hand-to-face gestures
　　Head tilted
　　Stroking of chin
　　Peering over glasses

Suspicion
　　Sideways glance
　　Touching of nose
　　Movement away from
　　　speaker

Nervousness
　　Throat clearing
　　"Whew" sound
　　Whistling
　　Cigarette smoking
　　Fidgeting in chair
Perspiration

anger, surprise, and boredom. But sometimes people
are so serious when they speak that others misinter-
pret their feelings as unfriendly or unhappy. They may
be happy but forget to notify their face.

The technical term for body language is *kinesics,*
from the Greek word *kinesis,* meaning motion. In the
1940s, anthropologist and linguist Ray L. Birdwhistell
began using movies to study his subjects. He labeled
the slightest perceptible tics or twitches *kines.* Larger
movements were called *kinemes;* raised eyebrows or a
wink would be put in this category. Combinations of
kinemes were *kinemorphs.* Birdwhistell determined
that these movements were largely subconscious.

Body language speaks loudly if we look as we listen
and note the signals a person sends along with the
words that are spoken. It is a language that can be far
more revealing than speech. Senator S. I. Hayakawa
of California, a former semantics professor, observed,
"In this age of television, image is more important than
substance." Communications specialist Marshall
McLuhan made a statement heard around the world in
the 1960s: "The medium is the message." He too
meant that image is more powerful than content.
McLuhan once explained that the real medium was the
"massage" of the eyes, what we see in a person. This
could be gestures, actions, even the expression or
character we observe.

So remember, we're communicating all the time,
even when we're not speaking. Try to be more aware
of other people's body language. When we observe

body movement, we're observing human behavior, human personality. This field of study is known as behavioral communications.

Watching for these signals is also known as listening between the lines. We've always done this unconsciously in the past. We can learn more and understand others better by being more aware of kinesics in the future.

This could also be called total listening—using the eyes, ears, and even the heart. One age-old saying is "Actions speak louder than words." Or, as the gurus of India proclaim by their lives of teaching and their example, behavior manifests belief.

8
Goals
for Understanding

*The most basic of all human needs
is the need to understand
and to be understood.*
> —Ralph G. Nichols

KEY QUESTIONS

Here are some key questions to ask yourself for understanding the information, ideas, and suggestions of others. These questions help you form goals or guidelines for personal improvement in listening.

- Do I listen to understand rather than spend the time preparing my next remark?
- Before agreeing or disagreeing, do I check to make sure I do understand what others mean?
- Do I try to summarize points of agreement or disagreement?

- Do I try to ask questions that result in a more informative answer than a yes or no?
- Do I try to encourage others to participate in the discussion?
- Do I guard against assuming I know what others mean or how others feel by asking them questions to assure understanding?
- Am I keenly aware of the other person's feelings when that person expresses a closeness and affection for me?
- When another's feelings are hurt, do I respond in such a way that I show sensitivity?

GOALS

To foster understanding, develop a deep respect for others. Speak to others first, and set a goal to listen to their response. This takes a strong conviction and lots of practice. Just listening to others and hearing them out makes them feel better. It often makes them feel important as well.

Set some goals to guide your inner feelings. Look for the good in others and show appreciation for people. Just listening to others is a sign of appreciation, but try to speak your positive feelings to others more frequently.

Review your strengths, weaknesses, and assets. Write out a list of your good points and then a list of your weaknesses as you and others who are close to you see them.

Try to create a positive climate around you at home

and the office for better communication, understanding, and cooperation. Develop trust of others and acceptance of them regardless of their faults. Listen totally to others and always level with them. As the sportscaster Howard Cosell says, "Tell it like it is." These steps are supportive and will breed agreement, initiative, free exchange, experimentation, and individual growth.

The opposite of these positive steps is to be too aggressive and defensive by always talking and evaluating others. There's too much control and even manipulation in an atmosphere of constant talk and criticism. Nonstop talkers and habitual criticizers create a defensive atmosphere and breed hostility, fighting, caution, and even game playing in others.

CORPORATE EARS

Every corporation, even a small organization, has two social systems. The first is symbolized by the head and signifies formal communication in the organization. This is management reaching objectives through plans, procedures, and policies. These are the factual, impersonal, formal messages that are communicated downward in the company.

The second corporate social system is symbolized by the heart. This represents the informal communication in every organization. This system is established by the employees to obtain satisfaction among themselves. It takes the form of car pools, coffee groups, unions, and social groups of many kinds.

117

The less the formal system is satisfying to them, the more people identify with the informal channels. The greater the gap between the two communications systems, the less effective is the organization in keeping morale high, establishing teamwork, motivating the employees, or winning cooperation.

To increase the effectiveness of the organization, the conflicts that exist between the formal and the informal systems must be eliminated. The best way to do this is to find out where the conflicts are. And the easiest way to do this is to have each executive call his or her subordinates together and ask them, "How can we do a better job?" "What can we do to improve communication?" Or "What can we do to improve our cooperation?" Then be silent and wait. Be patient. Let them know you're really interested in their ideas. Listen.

Answers will come slowly at first, but as your employees realize you are truly interested, they will speak up with a flood of ideas. Then you can ask, "How can we cut waste?" Or "How can we increase our profits?"

Strange, but true. The highest motivation can be achieved by just asking questions and listening to others. It's a nonfinancial incentive and it costs nothing but a little time. Most companies are already having regular meetings. So try this out.

DELPHI QUESTIONNAIRE

Before 1960, the Rand Corporation regularly scheduled discussion sessions between management and

On Disciplining the Tongue: Authors Unknown

"Listening is 50 percent of our education."

"The next best thing to brains is silence."

"The ears don't work until the tongue has expired."

"Those who know much usually say little, and those who say little usually know much."

"The keenest mind—honed to the sharpest condition—is generally accompanied by a tongue that does the least cutting."

"Be swift to hear and slow to speak."

"There are two kinds of people who don't say much—those who are quiet and those who talk a lot."

"Listen to others as you would have them listen to you."

labor representatives in an attempt to settle labor disputes. Usually the discussions were nonproductive. After 1960, Rand replaced the discussions with a detailed questionnaire, which was provided to the management and labor teams of negotiators. Each person was asked to answer all the questions completely and return the form by the following day.

People were asked about their mutual problems, needs, or objectives, but some questions sought out the deep convictions of the negotiators. Next, copies were made of every reply, and the sheets were circulated to every member of both sides so all the answers were available to everyone. Each member was urged to read and think over all the answers for a full week.

After a week, the same procedure was repeated. After a third week the procedure was repeated again. Each week the replies were different, but it was discovered that by the end of three weeks the concensus was as great as was possibly attainable. The representatives were then called into a meeting for discussion and satisfactory solutions were usually reached in a short time.

Prior to the Delphi Questionnaire, as Rand's questionnaire came to be called, active listening in a negotiating session was poor at best. Every person was prone to talk and not to listen to the other side. The Delphi method provided an alternative and proved to be the way to ensure sensible communication where each side listened to the opposition.

Again, listening to one another was the key to solving the disputes.

BENEFITS OF ACTIVE LISTENING

Active listening puts you in the forefront of action and makes you the channel for top-down and bottom-up communication. Active listening:

- Alerts you to opportunities before your competitors hear the whisper of the future.
- Develops insights impossible to managers who "don't have time to listen."
- Enlists the support of people above, around, and under you in the office hierarchy.
- Cements personal relationships with clients, colleagues, family, and friends.

120

- Reduces friction and resolves conflicts productively.
- Removes blocks and filters that get in your way.
- Ensures positive progress in planning, sales, and negotiations.
- Asserts your confidence, authority, and leadership better than words.
- Tells you when to act and how.
- Bridges gaps in understanding before they become crises.
- Keeps communications channels open.
- Prevents you from being cut off without the feedback you need to manage.
- Prevents people from going around you to someone who will listen.
- Gives you greater flexibility and confidence in every direction.

9
Applying Total Listening Techniques

Always listen to the opinions
of others. It may not do you
any good but it will them.
—Author Unknown

IN THE HOME AND COMMUNITY

A popular saying is "There's too much talk and not enough communication." The indication is that there's a great deal of chitchat taking place but little constructive conversation. People are so egocentric, everyone wants to talk, few want to listen. Yet, "the deepest principle in human nature is the craving to be appreciated," according to William James, early twentieth-century Harvard University psychologist. And there's hardly a better way to show interest in and appreciation of others than by listening to them in a concerned and total manner.

In their book *Egospeak,* Edmond G. Addeo and Robert E. Burger highlight the communications problem in the community and family in these words:

We hear it said that conversation is a "lost art," as if all we need to do to regain it is to practice it, or to try to think more before we verbalize, or to study a dozen other rules preached in innumerable volumes. Quite the reverse is called for, yet is increasingly ignored—listening. Unless we listen to what the other person is saying, we cannot reply to him effectively, nor can we take the next logical step in the conversation and permit it to flow freely and effortlessly.

We all love to talk but we want even more to be heard, to be listened to. In fact, we have a deep psychological need to be heard.

In business, community, or home conversations, remember the old proverb: "One pair of ears draws dry a hundred tongues." Follow the suggestions of the late Dale Carnegie, who urged two things: "Be a good listener; encourage others to talk about themselves," and "Let the other person do a great deal of the talking."

Use the better-listening principles outlined in this book to make yourself more welcome, more of a leader, more knowledgeable, more of a friend to others. Remember, if you're talking, you aren't learning. And don't forget that this book has highlighted the ways to be an expert listener.

Quotable Quotes on Listening and Silence

"A single conversation across the table with a wise person is better than ten years' study of books."
—Henry Wadsworth Longfellow

"*He who carefully listens, pointedly asks, calmly speaks, coolly answers, and ceases when he has no more to say is in possession of some of the best requisites of conversation.*"
—John Lavater

"*When in the company of sensible people, we ought to be doubly cautious of talking too much, lest we lose two good things—their good opinion and our own improvement; for what we have to say we know, but what they have to say we know not.*"
—Walter Colton

"*Give every man thine ear but few thy voice. Take each man's censure but reserve thy judgment.*"
—William Shakespeare

"*If you don't say anything, you won't be called upon to repeat it.*"
—Calvin Coolidge

You've learned six basic rules in the LADDER of listening success. Also, I presented four advanced techniques to HEAR and improve your listening anywhere.

I mention these ideas now to remind you that although I've given you the guidelines and techniques, practice is the best instructor. So review the key ideas and start practicing wherever you go.

The old saying is that charity begins at home. So

does good listening. Much of our time is spent at home with family members or roommates. Practice the art of questioning at home, and follow the questions with concerned listening. Use the rules and the distraction controls covered earlier. You will reap rich rewards while increasing your friendships and knowledge.

Teach these principles to others at home and in the community. Community includes church or synagogue, school, and clubs. And teach your colleagues and subordinates at work. Abe Lincoln said, "If you want to learn something teach it!" Only a small percentage of our population has ever had any training in listening. Teach others what you have learned in this book and you'll master the techniques yourself.

IN MANAGEMENT

The higher a manager goes in an organization the more he or she needs to learn from others to make decisions. So it's wise to involve subordinates early. Use skill in questioning to stimulate discussion and good ideas. Listening to an employee is the best tool a manager has for managing people.

Managers as well as clerks and secretaries in my management and communications courses over the years have said again and again, "My boss needs a course in listening." "My boss never listens to me." Or "My boss isn't interested in my ideas."

Listening to people is one of the most powerful nonfinancial incentives for motivating them. Make a list of the six LADDER rules and the four advanced techniques to HEAR better discussed previously. Put the list under the glass on your desk or someplace where you'll see it until you follow the guidelines unconsciously. Become a better manager by becoming a better listener. It'll be more fun, you'll learn more, and people will love you for it. You'll gain greater acceptance and be better able to motivate your subordinates.

The late psychologist Haim Ginott believed that what he called "the language of acceptance" can work miracles in human relationships. By listening to others without judging them, by accepting them, you help them see their situation objectively.

In his book *Teacher and Child,** Ginott offers this thought: "Whenever possible, I avoid telling [others] what to do and what not to do. Even when they ask for it, I postpone giving instant advice. I try to find out what they think about the situation and what alternatives they have considered. I encourage them to talk about their fears and hopes and to risk stating opinions and making decisions."

IN SELLING

One of the greatest changes that has taken place in our society is the big switch in recent years from the product-pushing, high-powered, fast-talking, city-slicker salesperson to a salesperson who questions the prospect or client and then listens.

*New York: Avon Books, 1972.

A salesperson who can't listen can't sell. The whole style of selling has changed to one known as participative selling. You ask questions to discover needs, problems, or objectives and listen to understand the prospect or customer.

Someone created this poem with the salesperson in mind, but the idea fits all of us:

> His words were few, and never formed to glisten.
> But he was a joy wherever he called
> You should have heard him listen.

Too many people, not just salespeople of the past, are senders only and not receivers. Listening is now called the key to sales success. The idea is to stop talking and start listening. To sell more, it's necessary to see things from the customer's point of view.

The person in control is the one who is asking the questions. While the customer is responding, the salesperson has time to listen, learn, and think.

INTERVIEWING

Another revolution comparable to the change in selling is the switch in business interviewing from telling to listening. For example, when interviewing prospects for a job in the past, interviewers would usually tell the prospect all about the job before asking questions. Then, as any bright applicant would do, the prospective employee would tailor all the answers to suit the description of the job. Many mistakes were made this way, too many. With today's high costs of hiring, personnel people have to be more effective in job placement.

The change in interviewing starts with the first words to a prospective applicant, and the emphasis is quickly put on making the interviewer the listener. A typical conversation might go like this: "Well, Miss Johnson, I know we didn't tell you much in the ad, but I'll be glad to tell you more about the position after I learn something about you. I'd like to know about your employment of the past five years and any periods of unemployment. Also what your duties consisted of on your last job. What kind of job you're interested in and what you liked or disliked about your past jobs. Take your time in answering."

The idea is to listen to what sort of communicator the person is and what sort of personality shows through. The content will be revealing even though guarded, but the real insight will be into the person's verbal abilities and personality.

It might take 10–15 minutes to answer those questions. That's fine. All that time the interviewer is learning about the applicant rather than selling the position first, as in the past. There is plenty of time later to explain the job if the applicant fits it. And the prospective employee won't be able to tailor the answers to the description of the job because the description comes last. And you will learn a great deal about the applicant without having to ask any of the many questions that might be considered intrusive. My whole point is that the switch in interviewing of any kind, even in sales, is to ask open-ended questions and listen rather than talk. And the techniques needed are explained in this book. Review the material a few times to master the methods suggested.

IN PERFORMANCE APPRAISAL

Job performance reviews, or in-depth appraisal sessions, have increased from once a year to two or three times a year in most corporations and to a quarterly basis in many companies. Once every three months is not too much in our fast-changing times. Besides, our enlightened society has discovered that people need constant feedback, crave appreciation, and need direction to improve and grow. In-depth counseling is essential, but regular daily counseling as possible is always welcomed by employees. Again, a shift to better listening by the managers providing the review is a big trend today.

Also, it benefits the employee to listen with an open ear, mind, and heart to all that is suggested for his or her improvement. Don't display the kind of problem demonstrated by one lad who told his wife when he got home, "Darling, I had my performance review today." She inquired, "How did it go?" And he said, "Great! My boss said I was doing much better in just about everything. He said I had only one problem area to work on." And his wife asked, "What area is that?" And he answered, "Listening. I think that's what he said."

All the steps in the appraisal process involve questioning and listening. Review the principles included in this book and apply them to counseling and appraisal.

AS A STUDENT

Listening to others and to ourselves is the first step toward improving our relationships with others. Listening actively is the way to learn and remember as well.

Singing star and movie actress Diana Ross said that her only regret in life was in education. She confessed, "I now say to myself: 'How come you didn't listen when you were in school?' You just never know what life has in store for you. The thing that saved me was that I was never afraid to ask questions, even if I was making a fool of myself."

In his book *Eloquence in Public Speaking,** Kenneth McFarland, the dean of American platform speakers, tells the story about the greatest teacher he ever had, Miss Georgia Brown of Caney, Kansas. McFarland explains, "She taught us arithmetic and reading, and she made us learn them. But she inspired us. She made us look beyond the narrow confines of our little town and up toward the stars. She used to say to me, "Kenneth, you're growing tall, but are you *thinking* tall? You know there is a ladder that goes right up through the roof of this schoolhouse? And you can climb up on it as high as you want to go. But the base of the ladder is in this school. This is where you

---

*New York: Random House, 1974.

get on it. This school provides your passport to wherever you want to go."

Follow Diana Ross's example and ask questions to learn and follow my LADDER principles to grow through total listening. Then you'll be able to follow Miss Brown's advice to "think tall," and you will be able to climb from school to anywhere you want to go.

AS A PARENT

Close the generation gap by spending more time with your children and with senior citizens in your family. In fact, make a pledge to spend more time talking with and listening to your spouse as well.

It will take a concerted effort by all members of the family to restore communication, understanding, and harmony in the home and with friends and neighbors. The essence of communication is participation. Unless someone listens, hears, and understands, there is no communication.

The Christophers of New York City, whose motto is "It is better to light one candle than to curse the darkness," circulated the following prayer in their *Christopher News Notes,* No. 195. It is used by permission to inspire each of us to make a firm resolution and a dedicated effort to listen to others:

Prayer to Be a Better Listener

We do not really listen to each other, God, at least not all the time. Instead of true dialogue, we carry on two parallel monologues. I talk. My companion talks. But what we are really concentrating on is how to sound good, how to make our points strongly, how to outshine the person with whom we are talking. Teach us to listen as your Son listened to everyone who spoke with him. Remind us that, somehow, you are trying to reach us through our partner in conversation. Your truth, your love, your goodness are seeking us out in the truth, love, and goodness being communicated. When our words are harsh, hostile, angry, we convey the very opposite of those qualities. Teach us to be still, Lord, that we may truly hear our brothers and sisters—and, in them, you. *Amen.*

Father Richard Madden, abbot at the Carmelite Fathers Monastery in Youngstown, Ohio, wrote out all the words that Christ spoke in his lifetime. Then he read them into a recorder at a normal speaking rate. He discovered that the total amount of time Christ spoke in public was 11 minutes. What a wonderful model for our new goal to talk less and listen more!

In fact, we can use the motto of the Salvation Army. Its founder, General William Booth, originated this one-word motto: OTHERS.

Finally, Meyer Friedman and Ray H. Rosenman, in their book *Type A Behavior and Your Heart,** issue a warning that a person who displays Type A behavior is more prone to having a heart attack than a person who avoids such behavior. Some of the key patterns of Type A behavior are:

1. Always rushing, not listening to your spouse.
2. Talking business while eating.
3. Talking too much and never listening to others.
4. Being impatient with others.
5. Losing your temper at work and home.
6. Showing hostilities, always fighting.

*Englewood Cliffs, N.J.: Prentice-Hall, 1961.

7. Hurrying others in their speaking.
8. Always interrupting.

Just think, by curbing these tendencies, you are also helping ensure a longer life.

Again, my purpose in this chapter has been to highlight some applications for the tools of listening and leadership included in this book. In time, with practice at home, in business, and in the community, you'll be astounded at your ability to listen actively and to remember accurately. Your personality will improve, your leadership ability will improve, and your friendships will increase and strengthen.

Remember, however, the sage advice of George Bernard Shaw "You have no more right to drink in conversation without contributing to it than you have to go into a store and take something without paying for it."

Now two thoughts in closing. One is a rhyme my mother repeated frequently in my school days in Minnesota:

> The wise old owl sat in an oak.
> The more he saw, the less he spoke.
> The less he spoke, the more he heard.
> Why can't we be like that old bird?

And finally, Christ's promise, as recorded by St. Mark in the Bible: "If any man has ears to hear, let him hear. And unto those who hear shall more be given."